IS IT SAFE?

Essays by Students in the San Quentin
College Program

Photographs by Heather Rowley

Edited by Jennifer Scaife

A publication of the Prison University Project

ISBN: 978-0-615-21247-0

For more information, please visit
prisonuniversityproject.org

Or write to us:
Prison University Project
Post Office Box 492
San Quentin, California 94964
info@prisonuniversityproject.org

CONTENTS

PHOTOGRAPHS

Introduction

Students wrote the personal essays featured here in a creative writing workshop I taught two years ago in the College Program at San Quentin. As a class, we discussed master essayists like James Baldwin, Joan Didion, and Richard Rodriguez; students then wrote their own stories to share with their classmates and me.

Self-disclosure takes courage in any writing workshop, for unveiling personal experiences can cause writers to feel vulnerable, sometimes even unsafe. Sharing a personal essay in prison—where people often guard their feelings and their memories closely, where privacy and physical safety are rarely taken for granted—can be a life-altering act.

In California's overcrowded prisons, two people frequently occupy a cell designed for one. People in prison can't help but intrude upon one another's personal boundaries, and yet often they remain strangers to one another. The personal essay workshop challenged students not only to get acquainted, but also to exchange critical feedback about one another's essays. Students had to trust each other not to respond with ridicule or hostility.

Gradually, students opened up. Some bonded over shared experiences of raising children, losing parents, struggling with disabilities. I know students worked hard to build a safe community in that classroom. The stunningly intimate essays collected here are proof.

Jennifer Scaife
Prison University Project

Artist Statement
Heather Rowley

Photographing men who are continually under surveillance, I am very aware that my camera holds the potential for even further intrusion. Some of these images offer little context, encouraging the viewer to see the men without the markers of imprisonment, while others pay special attention to the realities of their environment. During the past few years of shooting at San Quentin, I have taken pictures that allow students to present a self to the camera that they are proud of, photographing them at graduation, in class, studying, and participating in events such as the Poetry Slam. Students and I have explored the decisions photographers make when creating portraits and worked together so that they can play a leading role in how (or whether) to represent themselves on film. As a result, many of these photographs are collaborations between their ideas and my vision.

IS IT SAFE?

After the Flash of the Camera
Michael Bjorlin

I'm sixteen years old with a Kool-Aid smile and bright red hair, looking through cold hard bars from a jail cell on the Bonanza TV set. My mother is outside with her camera telling me how cute I look and cracking jokes to make sure I'm smiling when she takes the picture. As I'm sitting in that makeshift cell, I am curious about what it is like to live there, not knowing when or ever you would leave. That picture captures me locked up, but the smile says I'm walking out after the flash of the camera…

I'm seventeen years old with the same Kool-Aid smile and bright red hair, looking out of the open door of a squad car. My friends are standing outside with an officer and a Polaroid camera; it was a Polaroid scavenger hunt we were involved in. My friends were making jokes and laughing, saying how natural I looked sitting in the back seat of a squad car. As I smiled, they took the picture. I sat in the squad car, curious of how it felt to be cuffed up, people staring, pointing and talking about you. That picture captures me sitting in the backseat of a squad car, but the smile shows me getting out after the flash of the camera.

I'm twenty years old, with a saddened face and a balding head, looking out the window of the closed door of a squad car, outside the Sacramento airport. Policemen and the media are standing outside with their cameras, taking pictures and asking me questions. I'm sitting there cuffed up, embarrassed, and scared to death. There are people staring, pointing, and talking about me. The picture captures me sitting in a squad car, but the sadness on my face says I won't be getting out after the flash of the camera.

I'm now 36 years old, with a saddened, older face and a bald head, looking through cold hard bars from a prison cell in San Quentin State Prison. My mother, my friends, and the media are all outside with their cameras, waiting to take my picture. As I sit here, I feel lonely, caged up, withered and broken, not knowing when or ever I will be able to leave. What will this picture capture? What will my face show after the flash of the camera?

Fight for Life
Brent Brackett

I was trying to hide my face so no one would see. I was afraid of what they might think. They might make fun of me, they might laugh at me, they might tell someone. Once I started looking around, my fear of being seen was unimportant. The entire congregation was doing the same thing. It was impossible not to, no matter how hard I tried to hold it in. Under the conditions, it was the most natural and normal thing to do.

This was not the first time I cried for my friend. When Prop 66 was denied by voters, I cried for him. I cried because he was going to have to keep doing his life sentence. When I first met Ricky and found out he was doing a life sentence for being in possession of a stolen motorcycle, I was not only upset about him, but I was upset with the justice system. I already knew the justice system was unfair, because I was sent to prison for something I did not do. But a life sentence for a stolen motorcycle. That's ridiculous. What made it even worse was that he has a wife and daughter out there.

Ricky's relationship with his wife was re-established when there was hope that he might come home. His daughter was excited that her daddy was coming back and Ricky was excited to be going back home with his family. The voters bulldozed all of their excitement, though, when they voted no on 66. However rough

that may have been, it is all irrelevant considering Ricky's current situation. The situation that brought me and the entire church to tears.

In 2003, I noticed Ricky had a mole on his shoulder that looked like a raisin. Having seen what to look for regarding skin cancer, I informed him that he should get it checked out by a doctor. Unfortunately, there were a bunch of want-to-be doctors around us at the time who told him, "Man, that ain't no skin cancer, that's just a mole. Look, I got a bunch on my back," as he took off his shirt and showed us his moles. This was followed by a procession of other mole-toting amateur doctors discounting Ricky's malformed mole.

The mole went unchecked until two years later when it was diagnosed as malignant melanoma. At the time, no one took it to be very serious, including myself. I recall a conversation between Ricky and me in which I joked about his cancer. I told him people were going to start calling him "cancer boy," which I did. He was not offended by my words because neither of us thought skin cancer was anything to be worried about. Through joking, I was trying to soften the seriousness of the matter at hand, which is something I often do. I find it easier to laugh and make jokes about things that bother me. Unfortunately, this facetiousness has also gotten me into trouble. I had a girl I was dating who lost her kids. I joked that at least now she would save some money on food. She did not laugh and I did not get asked back into her house. I guess there are some things that should not be joked about. For instance, when Ricky's cancer progressed.

One day when Ricky was in the shower he found a lump under his arm. Concerned, he went to the doctor and found out he had a tumor on his lymph node. I could not help being concerned and worried for my friend. I have another friend who was going through the same thing and it was tearing him up. It was sucking his life away, his body was deteriorating more each day. He was nothing but skin and bones; people joked he looked like the walking dead. It hurt me to think that Ricky was going to have to go through the same torment.

After the surgical removal of the tumor, he was given treatment in the form of 20 million units of interferon, which occurs naturally in the body, but at that mega dose it will bring any man enough misery that he will want to die. To everyone's dismay, the interferon was not working. Things got worse.

One day I saw Ricky walking and he did not look very happy. I approached him and gave him a big hug. I asked him what was wrong and he explained to me that he was dying. I thought to myself, Oh, here we go again. That is of course until he told me that he was coughing up blood and had a tumor in his lung. I was immediately struck with concern and sadness. All of the small, meaningless problems in life no longer seemed important. The jokes stopped. The realization that I might lose a good friend took control of my emotions. I felt like crying but held back because men are not supposed to cry in prison.

I learned this lesson early, my first time in jail when my girlfriend broke up with me. I was laughed at and made fun of. A few fellow inmates pulled up chairs next to the phone where I was crying to my girlfriend. First they brought me a roll of toilet paper and then sat there rubbing their fists on their eyes, making "whaa whaa" noises. Very embarrassing. I decided that I would never be seen crying in jail again. With everything going on with Ricky, I knew that was going to be a difficult task.

The reason Ricky was coughing up blood was soon found out to be a tumor in his lung. With the worthless medical conditions in prison, it will take a miracle to cure Ricky's cancer.

A special Mass was held for Ricky at church the following Sunday so the congregation could pray for him. This is where I could not control my emotions and cried for the first time in many years. At first, I was a little embarrassed because I was crying, but then I just cried, I could not stop it no matter what. I cried for my friend, I cried for his daughter, I cried for his wife, I cried for his family, I cried for myself. At 36 years old, my friend was too young to die. I hope and pray that my friend wins this battle for his life, proving that life is not completely unfair.

Editor's Note: Ricky Earle died on March 8, 2007.

Take a Bite
Yu Chen

"Man, you can't handle this."

"Oh, yes I can."

I was at a former schoolmate's party and once again witnessed a contest of manhood.

A fresh orange-reddish pepper dangled from the first man's fingers. It was about one inch across and resembled a mini sweet bell pepper except for its pointed tip.

"Look. I owe you a case of beer if you chew up this pepper and swallow it," he dared.

The second man took the pepper and put it into his mouth without hesitation. He chewed. He was OK… But that lasted only a few seconds. Then he yelped, sending the mauled pepper flying. He hissed and panted while his face turned crimson, his eyes watered, and his nose ran. Friends handed him cups of cold water and milk with laughter. He was still huffing and puffing half an hour later. Apparently, he had had no idea about habañeros.

I started to eat chili peppers regularly when I was five years old. My parents enjoyed peppers with moderation. We used green peppers of milder varieties as vegetables and more pungent ones only for seasoning. My tolerance for capsaicin increased over the years.

Occasional overconfidence or carelessness had taught me a healthy respect for peppers, especially unfamiliar ones. One time I was duly punished for failure to wash my hands thoroughly after handling cut peppers. The burn on my hands lasted for more than two days.

Luckily, the earlier lessons had spared me the agony experienced by the man who did not win the case of beer. Though I considered myself pepper-hardy, I had resisted all temptations for such bets, even before I knew anything about habañeros. It was not easy, considering my weak bench press and my dislike for alcohol. With peppers, I might have a chance…

I first heard about habañeros from a Guatemalan co-worker and read everything I could get hold of about them. Some pepper experts rate the habañeros, *Capsicum chinensis*, as the hottest pepper in the world, about 40 times as hot as the popular jalapeño.

I have no idea where the chinensis part comes from because habañeros, like all other chili peppers, originate from the Americas, not China. In fact, habañeros are generally unknown to the average Chinese. In China (perhaps the whole East Asia) varieties of what is called the Thai pepper in the US are the hottest peppers commonly available in markets, under different names in different regions. Thai peppers are very hot, but not in the same league as habañeros. I have seen many he-men, whose confidence builds on Thai peppers, taking up the habañero challenge and getting burned in both mouth and pocket.

Habañeros are stealthy. A slice the size of a penny is difficult to spot in a stir-fry, yet it sets the whole dish on fire. The slice itself still packs the distinctive habañero sting even after being cooked with and diluted by other ingredients. I, for one, am glad to have heard about them before trying them, because with habañero, it is too easy to bite off more than one can chew.

Where Have All the People Gone?
Randall Countryman

Growing up in the countryside of Southern Ohio offered little potential for developing many friendships. In farm country, the houses didn't set right on top of one another, or even next-door. Our closest neighbor was an old couple a mile away on a lonely stretch of road, one lane wide, whose black pitch softened and bubbled in the hot sun. Underfoot the bubbles would pop and my sneakers left a trail through the tar and out into the middle of that ribbon cut through the cornfields and hardwood forests, on my way to investigate a frog, snake or other unsuspecting creature pressed into the pavement after making a bad decision to cross the road at the wrong time. It didn't matter if they looked both ways or not, some just didn't escape the proverbial train. I used to mow the old people's lawn and every Christmas my family would take them a big basket of fruit which contained several varieties of jams, crackers, meats and cheeses. Seeing their wrinkled faces with toothless grins light up, and the moistening in their eyes made an otherwise cold, snowy day glow with warmth.

Despite the seclusion of country life, I made acquaintances and friendships with kids from school. We played baseball together, hunted, fished and swam in the creeks and ponds that dotted the landscape. Our parents often invited one another over for cookouts and family events. My best friend Rusty and I became inseparable after the second grade and the two of us could find more mischief than ten boys. Actually we didn't have to go find chaos, we were like small satellites or planets that had our own gravitational pull and it knew that. Trouble had an uncanny ability to track us down. I would hate to have to play hide and seek with it, because I would surely be discovered instantly.

Rusty was the kind of kid who was going to have it relatively easy in life. He had natural good looks: dirty blond hair, sparkling white teeth and just the right bone structure and facial features that would ensure he wouldn't have a lonely life. He often experimented with hair styles; short and spiked, shoulder length, parted in the middle and feathered back, or parted on the left, and he even showed up to school one morning with a perm. None of these alterations negatively affected his appearance. I on the other hand was often introduced to the business end of my mother's barber scissors. That certainly didn't help my looks any.

We went on great expeditions through the hills and woods, our backpacks full of bologna and cheese sandwiches, little bags of potato chips, cigarettes and cans of beer stolen from our parents. We explored abandoned homesteads and barns and stuffed our packs with old books that had yellowed, dog-eared pages, lanterns, rust encrusted tools, cookware and anything else that appeared to have some measure

of value to it. Our idea of valuable treasure was pretty liberal. I remember on one of our excursions we returned with nothing more than a sack full of groundhog bones. We cleaned them in a solution of bleach and warm water, scrubbing them with an old toothbrush. Metal coat hangers were used for support as we methodically reconstructed the skeleton and mounted it on the best piece of wood I could find. That board just happened to be one of the shelves from my mother's china cabinet, but I didn't break any of her dishes and I left them neatly stacked on the counter, which I thought should have accounted for something, but it didn't. See what I mean by trouble tracking us down?

I found one dilapidated house in particular to be spooky. More than spooky actually, it was downright scary. It was an old two-story house, probably over a hundred years old, and had nearly fallen in on itself by the time we stumbled across it. The front door leaned awkwardly, hanging on one hinge where there had once been three. It creaked eerily as we brushed past it to gain entrance into the creepy recesses of what could have very well been in my mind a haunted mansion. Plaster from the ceiling had fallen in powdery chunks and mingled with the layer of dust on the floor where we stood. I wondered who was the last living person to stand on this sagging floor. The hair standing up on the nape of my neck made me feel pretty certain that the dead had walked where I now stood, and not too

Mike Bjorlin on the yard

long ago either, maybe even last night.

The planks groaned and threatened to give way under our weight. Here and there, vines and plants had pushed their way between the boards and basked in the shafts of sunlight that had found holes in the roof and the clapboard sides of the house. The floor, or what was left of it, was also littered with broken glass, pieces of torn clothing and most troublesome of all, a little red shoe that was lying on its side next to a ragged, gaping hole. The sneaker looked to be about the right size to fit a four or five year old and was partially eaten away. I could see the puncture marks caused by teeth—no, fangs, sharp canine fangs. A rational mind would deduce they were probably caused by some animal that lived in the woods and had chosen it as a chew toy, intrigued by the odor, as it used the room for shelter during a storm. All sense of rationality had departed from me the moment I entered the house and I just knew the red color on the shoe wasn't natural, it was blood and the animal that had chewed the shoe was not of the ordinary cuddly forest variety, it was an evil beast that had ripped through the sneaker while the child was still in it. I wanted nothing more than to leave that place way before nightfall when unknown things lurked and patrolled the hallways. There wasn't anything of value except an old wire bird cage by the door; we took it with us. At the last moment before crossing the threshold to exit the crumbly building, I dashed back to the wide-open mouth in the floor and snatched up the tennis shoe and stuffed it into my pack. Perhaps it would be useful in solving a missing person case in the future. Perhaps some day I would be a detective.

I miss those treasure hunts and adventures and I would even go back into that house right now, haunted or not, just to relive the experience and enjoy the childhood friendship with my pal. I haven't heard from my friend, Rusty, in over twenty years. In my isolation from the real world, I get nostalgic and become curious of the lives that have touched me somewhere deeply. Did I impact them in the same way? Am I alone in my thoughts of what has become of them? We lose people in our big, fast-paced world. We become what all the little events of days stacked upon days make of us. Life as a whole is the finished piece from a proficient artist or poet. Each experience is but one stroke of the pen, its ink splashed across the page. Every poem is a masterpiece, regardless of the labor involved in its creation. There are no mistakes, only the use of an artistic license to vary the work. Stories are often intertwined and share the same space of parchment between the binding. The book of life with its pages pressed together opposite of one another, allows them to participate in an alternate landscape, get to know each other and possibly build friendships. They inevitably get lost in each other and within themselves.

That is what I mean when I say we lose people. We

get on with our own business of living and waiting to cease to be. Everything we have shared is boxed away and stored somewhere out of sight where our sounds and smells are kept, until we are reminded of instances of time, of people and of places. I am not speaking of losses due to freak accidents, disease or old age coming to collect when rent's due. I write of the friendships and relationships we've encountered and promised never to forsake. The same ones that for whatever reason get broken and forsaken. We lose people and wonder where they have gone.

Accepting Things As They Are
Henry Edward Frank

"I want to be known for two things. The first is that I was the best Christian I could be and the second is that I was the best Indian I could be," Ada Mae Frank, my grandmother, would always say. To all that knew her, they remember her as just that. She knew the Bible and spoke Yurok fluently. She knew hymns as well as traditional songs. She knew of nature and of heaven. A delicate and complicated dance between two worlds, which never collided within her. I hope I am remembered by the people who know me that I was the best Indian I could be.

Most of the Natives I grew up around did not wear regalia, they as I wore clothes and necklaces made of gold and silver. Half of my family went to church. I prefer the sweat lodge. I can't stand the taste of abalone or eel (my tribal survival foods). I know my heritage and I have been taught and learned traditional songs, dances prayers and knowledge. I have lived on the Rez in Wietchpec and in Hoopa. Just because my name isn't Hawk Flying at Highnoon over Twelve Deer Drinking at the River as an Otter Swims By and I was named Henry Edward Frank changes nothing.

Furthermore, if I tell the world that I am a savage, or if I tell one person that I am Indian, or if I tell no one that I am a Native American, or if I didn't know that I was from the PU-LIK-LAY nation would not

Brent Brackett

Yu Chen in class

change the blood flowing through my veins or the dna in my genes. I am Yurok because I was born Yurok.

I was recently asked at the San Quentin Fall Pow-Wow, located in the visiting room, by a young woman from San Francisco state, "How do you maintain your identity as a Native American while incarcerated?" I found this question absurd, as she was a skin too. "I do not have to maintain anything, act a certain way, believe a certain things, wear my hair long, or be classified by the administration as an AMI within this prison system. I maintain my identity by breathing. Anything I do, think, or say will be Indian, because that is what I am," I thought to myself. I didn't voice these thoughts because I didn't want to be perceived as hostile or bitter from my incarceration. I simply answered, "I was born Indian and nothing has changed since." She smiled as she jotted my quote down and responded with, "that's cool."

I consider myself lucky, because my brother and I were raised "Indian." I knew I was a Yurok before I knew I was a boy. Being raised "Indian" is probably the same as being raised any other nationality. My parents, aunts, uncles, grandmother and their friends were proud to be Yurok. Based upon the characteristics of my loved ones, I learned that being a Yurok meant: Loving your children unconditionally, hiding your drugs in a pair of boots in the corner of your room underneath a pile of clothes so your mother would not find it. Compromising some of your happiness so your

loved ones could be happy as well, children were to be seen and not heard. Spending time with your family because you want to, drinking unconditionally until you pass out. No matter what you are doing or how old you are, you checked in with your mother so she knew you were still alive. Indians lived in apartments in Eureka, slept on the ground in Star Wars and Alf sleeping bags in Weitchpec, lived in San Francisco in an apartment where I had to walk down the hall to use the restroom. We ate at a table at the apartment. We went out to restaurants. We ate hunks of salami, cheese and sourdough bread while drinking Welch's white grape juice on a pier at Fisherman's Wharf. We attended church. We attended Brush dances and Pow-Wows. We attended school, we dropped out of school, and we graduated from the University of San Francisco with a Bachelor's of Arts degree. Everything I saw my family do, everything I heard them say, everything I saw them eat and every reaction, response and emotion displayed contributed to my ideology of what it meant to be Indian. Now, everything I say, do and think is what an Indian is.

I do not beat my clothes against a rock, I do not, nor even have a ridden horse. It hasn't ever rained after I finished dancing. I do not wear a loincloth and I do not greet people with "How." I don't throw a net in the Klamath River to catch salmon. I do not live my life on "Indian time," which is a sense of time of when I get there, I get there and when it gets done, it gets done. I don't wear moccasins nor do I have a desire to. I do not speak my native tongue, but I do speak perfect English. I wash my clothes at a laundromat. I drive a car or ride a bike. I wear "American" clothing and I am comfortable. I greet people with "Hello" or "What's up, dog?" I purchase my salmon at Safeway. I wear a Timex digital watch so I am not late to appointments and I get things done by the designated deadlines. Finally, I wear triple E wide New Balance tennis shoes. I do practice my Native American culture (like my grandmother) but I have also assimilated to American culture. Still, it does not take away from my Red Heritage.

In prison I am identified by other prisoners and staff as an injun, because I sweat and wear beads. I have long dark hair and I hang out with mostly other Indians. They have seen me play the drum and heard me sing songs. They have seen me at Pow-Wows and that my pigment is consistent with what color an Indian should be. As most Natives know, all these things do make me an Indian.

The things I do believe in are not ways for me to show the world that I am indigenous to this land. It's just who I am. I sweat in the sweat lodge because that is where I feel most comfortable, most connected with God and where I have gained the most understanding. A place where I learn who I am and sit before God in my truest form. I am a spirit as every other living being in existence is a spirit. Due to this understanding I know I am no greater nor any less, but equal to all life.

I play the drum because I like the sound and the feeling of the drum. It connects all the generations before me and the generations that will come after me. As I pound the same sounding beat of the past and of the future into existence, interweaves our spirit as I sit here in the present. I offer up songs with my drumming because I understand that each song has power and when I sing them, I am calling upon its power and directing it. Songs are prayers and there is a time and place to sing each song.

My pigment changes shades with the seasons. During the summer I am the color of bronze and during the winter I attain an orangish red color with a copper tint. Mentioning my skin: I have tattoos, which do identify me as a wagon burner. Again, I did not get my tattoos to show the world that I am a Native American. They all have meaning that remind me of why I travel on this Redroad to the Creator. The Hawk in the center of my back swooping down for a landing with a salmon in her talons, which has a Yurok design (which I use to symbolize the Universe) for his eye, reminds me that no matter where I end up, I will be provided for. The PU-LIK across the top of my back translates into "Down River" in English, and reminds me that no matter how many times I have to tell my incarcerators that I am J-80928, I know where I came from and how my existence came to be. The ROK-CIHM KU

Randall Countryman

Henry Frank's speech for the Day of Peace

TE-NU-MO-NOK, translates into "Trust the Spirits," which came to me when I needed a sign that I was not on this earth by randomness or that I was not at this moment in time, occupying this space by accident. The Creator did not fail me and I have greater faith that I am walking the path I am supposed to, because He reached down and blessed me and gave me a spirit calling song. I sing this song during the first round of the Sweat Lodge ceremony. Finally, I have a red tailed hawk gliding at full wing span, soaring from my left side of my back, behind the center hawk, to the right side, which reminds me that I am free, no man-made structure can retain or restrict my spirit.

I am proud of being a Native American and that I am connected with nature and my understanding of the divine, all add to who I am. My upbringing, education, hardships and celebrations, my joys and pains, my wisdom and ignorance, and just living and experiencing life add to who I am. None of these factors make me a Yurok Indian. I am the best savage I can be, because I have no choice, I can be nothing else.

The King's Project
Ricky Gaines, II

Uncle Freddy, who is the oldest of Grandma Mattie's eight children, would always jokingly tell me that he had a son my age, and that he could beat me up.

"Lil' Rick, my son Chico is my junior like you are to your Dad, and if I tell him to get on you, he will do it," Uncle Fred would say.

"Well, what's the problem, go and get him," I'd shoot back at my uncle, trying to sound serious. Uncle Freddy loved me and I loved him. He'd always find some creative way for me to go places with him, like to the store, business seminars, or to odd jobs around the city with him. I think that he felt guilty about not having his son Chico living with him.

"Hey son, come and ride with me to Raley's. We need to go buy some barbeque sauce and sodas for Momma," he said on a day when the family was all over to my Grandmother's house for a family gathering. We live in Pittsburg, California; a small town-city in the Bay Area, near Richmond, where everyone knows each other or their families. Grandma Mattie has four boys and four girls, of which my father is the youngest son. There's Uncle Freddy, Carl, Marvin, and Richard. On the girls' side, there's Aunty Mary, Evonne, Mallory, and my favorite Aunty, Rosie. Rosie is what we call in our family "the famous aunt" because she is a well-known musician, and she has lived in Minneapolis,

Minnesota at Prince's estate, while she was a member of his band. "Diamonds and Pearls" was one of the hit songs that made her famous with Prince, so we have always been extremely proud as a family of her success.

I eventually met my cousin Chico many years later when I moved in with my Grandmother and started junior high school. It was three months into the school year, and as I walked the halls of Central Junior High, all I could think about was that my cousin Chico also went to that school. Classes were in session already, and I was late because the principal had given my grandmother and me a brief orientation of the school. Walking through the halls, I was looking inside every classroom as I passed, hoping to get a glimpse of my cousin. It's funny, because actually I didn't really believe I would see him. Then, suddenly I saw a face that I didn't immediately recognize, but something in my gut told me by his return stare that I should've known him. I paused, he stood up and we both just stood still, staring at each other.

"Rick, is that you – cousin?" he said with a big grin on his face. I just stood there smiling from ear to ear, lost in thought. He looks a lot like me, dark complexion, slim build, and he's handsome, I thought. "Chico, what's up, cousin?" I said as I made an open arms gesture with my hands. By this time he had totally disrupted the classroom's atmosphere of learning, and he was halfway out the door. Greeting

me with a solid handshake and a warm bear hug, I could tell that he was as happy as I was to finally meet him. We were both twelve years of age, and we had so much catching up to do.

Even though he lived on the other side of town, we were inseparable because nothing could keep up away from each other. As we got older, we bought an apartment together and we continued to be inseparable. If you saw me, you saw him, or knew that he'd be arriving soon.

Chico showed me around school, introducing me to people he knew as if I was an ambassador from out of the country or something.

"Ah Mo'dean, this is my cousin who I've been telling you about, Ricky. He's here now so you know that it's on," he'd say. I didn't have a clue to who any of these people were, but I could tell that they were checking me out, and trying to size me up. "Robin, this here is my cousin Rick, he's in your homeroom class, so make him feel comfortable, okay?" he said to this pretty young lady with a tremendous smile on her face. She didn't say a word, just kept smiling. I'm looking and smiling myself at first, but after a few minutes, the young lady was still smiling, and now I'm thinking to myself, this girl is crazy! So I eased on down the hall, nodding to my cousin to bring his butt on.

That day in junior high school was like the day of a brand new life for both of us. There was no turning

Ricky Gaines

John Hart supporting a friend at the poetry slam

away from each other from that moment on, because I think we were anticipating meeting one another and coming together. People were always mentioning me to him, or him to me, and we hadn't even seen each other yet. So the build-up to the moment we met was huge, and we both couldn't wait. I'll never forget the day when I was called into the captain's office while incarcerated.

"Mr. Gaines, your sister called and I'm sorry to inform you that your brother had an accident," he said, trying to measure his words. I was not even registering what he was saying, because I knew that I didn't have any brothers.

"Apparently your brother took a trip to the NBA All-Star game, and there was an accident later that night. Your brother Fredrick Gaines was shot once in the stomach and he later died at the hospital," the captain announced, this time looking intently at me, checking for my reactions to his words. In my mind, at first I was thinking that someone back at home must have really wanted me to call home, so they had called the prison with a bogus story about a brother I never had. Then, when I heard the name "Fredrick Gaines," my heart dropped to my stomach, and now I began to shake my head – as if to say, "You cannot be correct, that's not true. I had just spoken with my cousin Chico nearly a week ago on the phone, and he was happy about his music career which was taking off for him." I didn't move, just stood there looking at

this person who I had never even seen before, telling me about my cousin, like he knew the both of us. I wanted to get out of that office as fast as I could, so I turned away, feeling the tears welling up in my eyes.

"I need to get on the telephone," I said as I looked back at the captain. I didn't wait for a response as I started out of his office and back to my housing unit. Outside, the air was cool and the night was clear. It seemed like I was walking outside of my body because I could see myself moving at a steady pace but could also feel my eyes burning from the tears.

Memories began to flash into my mind, of my cousin and me, and I began to replay conversations we had over the years in my head. The first time we met came rushing back into my mind. It seems like so many lives have been touched by my cousin and me, and it's not the same without him around. I dialed the number to my sister's house, but when she answered and accepted the collect call, the sound of her voice took away my breath. I could not even speak. My sister understood the emotions I was consumed by, so she talked and talked, filling me in to every last detail. I was saddened and angered by my cousin's untimely death, because he had totally changed his life and was being a responsible father, making music for a living, and staying away from the streets. To think that he went to a public event like the All-Star Game and was murdered by some person who shot into a crowd of people just makes me mad at the senselessness of urban violence. It taught me lessons that I can never forget about life, and I hope to eventually build a non-profit business for children who have been affected by gun violence in my cousin's honor in the near future. It was April of 2004 and Chico was 28 years of age.

Chicken Adobo
Michael C. Gallardo

Hundreds of people come to San Francisco's annual Adobo cook-fest to get a taste of this famous dish. It is world famous, at least that's how it seems when anywhere I go someone asks about it. Then maybe people just connect it to Filipinos. People see Filipinos and they think of adobo.

A Filipino party isn't complete without it. When pinoys invite their friends and families to their homes, they will be asked, "Will there be some adobo?" In lunchrooms in workplaces around the world, we are bombarded with questions like, "How's the adobo?" or *"Is that adobo?"* While most people may feel offended or awkward to be identified with food, say like Mexicans with burritos, or Japanese with sushi, I am proud to be recognized with my favorite dish, which carries so much of our history.

It's very durable and will last forever. "It's because of the vinegar," my mother once said. While in high school studying Philippine History, I learned that during the Spanish revolution villagers handed out adobo wrapped in banana leaves to the guerillas as they headed to the mountains. Not knowing when they would be able to eat, with its durability, it was the best they could have that would last. Imagine that, my favorite food goes back to the Spanish occupation, during the time when there was no refrigeration

James Hayes

available. I remember when my parents would leave for the country every month, mother would yell out, "There's adobo in the fridge." Then they were gone, leaving us kids alone for the weekend. The last minute announcement assured us that there was food while they're gone. After they left, my brothers and I would run back to the kitchen and there it was, three healthy bowls of the best chicken adobo.

It's easy to make and takes about ten to fifteen minutes. I once heard of it as the Philippines' Mac and Cheese, although it takes more than throwing the chicken in boiling water. Mac and Cheese is not the American national dish, but it was a famous meal among students while I was in college in San Jose, mainly because it only takes a few minutes to prepare. Growing up, I always knew when mom's day was hectic: there would be a bowl of steaming chicken adobo for dinner. So don't be surprised to see pinoys feeling neglected for having it too often, since it only takes a few minutes to make. "Better than leftovers for dinner," my mother would answer back when my sisters and brothers complained for having it again. I just kept giving my mom the thumbs up. It's best served with fresh steamed rice and if you ask my older brother, a little banana ketchup wouldn't hurt it, but he puts banana ketchup on everything. I leave it as it is. I like the taste of vinegar and soy sauce with garlic to linger in my mouth longer.

Fry the chicken first, in oil and a little bit of garlic, until golden brown. Then mix the vinegar and soy sauce in, two parts soy sauce and one part vinegar. For extra flavor, throw in some bay leaves and whole black peppercorns a few minutes before the heat is turned off. Use just enough vinegar and soy sauce to have it somewhat dry; a little more than enough will give you more juice to mix with your rice. I'll take it either way.

Ahh, the aroma of vinegar mixed with soy sauce is in the air. Mom's been busy at work; I ought to thank someone for that.

Felix Lucero

Michael McKenzie

Lies on the Big Yard
John Hart

As far back as I can remember I was always a big dude. I say big, but what I really mean is fat. Part of the problem is I love to eat! A lot of kids I knew growing up were picky and would only eat certain things. Not me, I'd eat anything, all of it, and hopefully more. Kids can be cruel and I endured my fair share of being teased. As a youngster living in the ghetto I learned to fight at a young age so I wasn't teased that much, but deep down I wrestled with confidence over my weight.

As I look back on my life I realize I grew up poor. I never knew any better growing up, though, because all the kids from my town were in the same boat. I grew up around outlaws, rebels, drunks, dope dealers, and motorcycle gangsters. My neighborhood, a ghetto in Del Paso Heights, never produced college graduates, student athletes, homecoming queens, or anything positive that I can remember. The only graduates I can recall were those going from juvenile hall to prison. It wasn't till many years of being removed from these surroundings that I realized that I was so disadvantaged. Being around people who come from better places has always made me feel a little uncomfortable.

There's an old saying from Del Paso Heights that goes something like this: Q: "What do you get when you put all the girls of Del Paso Heights together?" A: "A full set of teeth!" While this is a joke there is some truth to it. Girls from the hood were rough and tough, cold and ruthless, my kind of girls! They would punch or stab you just as fast and hard as the fellas. There's a term we coined to refer to the homegirls: "North Sac Nasties!" Yes, I was part of the problem. These were the girls I knew and loved growing up. They were the girls I felt comfortable with, the kind I'd be proud to bring home to Mom, the type I felt I deserved.

When I came to prison I was more of a boy than a man. At this point in my life I've been locked up nearly as long as I was free. All my memories from the street are distant ones. I've lived in the company of convicts for a long time. My best friends are all killers. The people who I hang out with, those who I identify with most, have no respect for authority, the rules of society, they hate cops, and would rather rob a bank than work in one. I can't say that I'd want many people in here as my neighbor on the street. The prison yard conversations consist of people sitting around trying to convince one another that they were once about something. We engage in safe topics like sports, the weather, war stories from the streets, and other shallow subjects designed to avoid the real issues—that is, we are bums, we're ignorant, have no power, that we're essentially emasculated. We often exaggerate and fill in the blanks to make ourselves look good, or to make the story better. Sometimes we forget and put in whatever makes the story more interesting. Many tales are complete fabrications, out and out lies. We all know this, accept it, even embrace it because story time is a good way to kill time. When a person takes the time to ponder these truths he becomes aware that his everyday existence is not a healthy place to be. Having been submerged in this culture for so long makes me sadly comfortable in it, and not very comfortable outside of it.

Fifteen years into a life sentence I have toured the state's prison system. I've done time up north, down south, level 4, level 3, and now here at San Quentin I'm doing level 2 time. My comfort zones have consisted of ghettos, "North Sac Nasties," and a bunch of lying assed convicts living under self-delusions. I've been securely tucked away from other rungs on the social ladder since the day I was born. Fast forward me to this current place and I am, for the first time in my life, being exposed to people and ideas that are completely foreign. Having regular contact and interactions with college graduates, college professors, and 'normal' people talking about normal things has placed me all the way outside my zones of comfort. All the events of my life have not prepared me for this and the result is something I never really knew: self doubt!

The Romance That Began by Twilight
James Hayes

I observed her standing there by the swimming pool in the back yard of this house I was invited to for a party; the only words that crossed my mind were "Good Lord!!!" Her beauty was so captivating that it practically took my voice away. Any other time I would've had a response to such a situation, but at that moment I could only stand there in the den where the partying was taking place, surrounded by people talking, flirting and dancing together listening to the music which was playing.

I was very aware of my surrounding and the activities that were going on, but the lady had me mesmerized with her beauty, the way she was standing by the pool which was the brightest color of blue I've ever seen. It coordinated with the clothes she had on, which were a turquoise silk dress with spaghetti string straps that crossed in the back to show off the most perfect shoulders and back I had ever seen on a woman; the shoes she wore matched her dress. She had a gold chain with a black opal medallion hanging around her neck that gave her appearance a more glamorous allure. I was able to see most of her appearance, because she did turn slightly to the side where you could make out certain details that I couldn't see precisely.

What really caught my attention, besides her striking beauty, was the way she was looking up at the sky or

Terrell Merritt

William Packer

stars like they were going to give her advice. The more I watched her I could tell this was a woman with serious questions on her mind that needed answers. I on the other hand had to get my movement back, because I was momentarily paralyzed.

As I was proceeding toward her I noticed she looked familiar to me, and that's only because I hadn't gotten a very good front view of her, but yet still I knew she was beautiful; it was in the way she stood there so gracefully with the attitude of someone commanding respect, because she earned it with her personality.

I approached this lady with a strange feeling in my heart; not from lack of confidence. I had myself together: I was wearing a smoked gray shark skin suit, tan silk shirt, tan kangaroo skin shoes, and my hand and neck looked like a jewelry store display case. Yes, my appearance was appropriate for the occasion; so what was this feeling in my heart?

I came up on her from the side, my first statement to her was would she mind if a gentleman interrupted the thoughts of such a beautiful lady, "because you appear to have some serious thoughts going through your mentals, meaning mind." She turned around from hearing my suggestion, and said point-blank, "Why don't men ever own up to their action and responsibilities?" That statement and response caught me off guard, because it was the very first time anyone ever mentioned something of that magnitude to me

upon first meeting me. Her response shocked me, I really thought she was being sarcastic at first until I read the expression on her face; she was serious.

I was just about to respond when I realized I know this beautiful woman and she knew me, we had been dodging each other for more than 10 years. It started when we were in high school, we would see each other at school events. She went to Overfelt and I to Silver Creek, in San Jose, California. She ran track and field and I played football.

One evening after school, I saw Alicia walking from school. She was looking so lovely as I rode by her in my 65 Chevy Impala low rider; she acknowledged that she saw me by waving her hand for me to pull over. I parked my car up on the sidewalk, got out and asked Alicia what was up with her, and if she would mind if I walked her home. She replied that yes I could walk her home, but what about my car, since I left it running on the sidewalk.

I told her no one was going to touch my ride, because the whole town knew who that car belonged to. Anyway as we were talking her mother pulled up on us in her car and called Alicia to it. She said, "Alicia, is that the boy they call Memphis?" Alicia said, "yes" and that's when her mother told her she couldn't talk to me because I was a gangster, and she didn't want her to associate with me period. She made Alicia get in the car with her, and they left.

Every time Alicia saw me after that she would always run away saying, "My mother says I can't talk to you." But to my surprise she had always had a strong desire to be with me, because she always heard good things about me regardless of the life-style I was living. And that's why we were dodging each other, I because I didn't want to hurt her in any way and her, because of her mother. With life's obstacles in front of us I'm proud to say that evening in Milpitas, California became the turning point in my life.

We talked for hours out there beside the pool about her reason for being out that night, because she wasn't the type of woman who went out by herself. She told me she needed to get out and do some thinking, and that her prayer was answered by seeing me that night, because she had seen me in her dreams many times. I looked at this woman who resembles Jada Pinket and Lisa Bonet; I saw the sincerity in her eyes.

That night I also answered her initial question, "Why don't men ever own up to their actions and responsibilities." I told her how most of them are immature cowards who draw their strength from women with emotional blackmail, and they lack the confidence of dealing with people being themselves, so they create illusions to captivate your attention until they lose control of that illusion and you are able to see through the deceit. She had tears in her eyes, because she knew I had told her the truth.

That lady on a warm summer night in 1986 won my heart. She became my wife in 1988; she was that soul-mate one searches for in life and I'm sure of it. True love I know.

Ray Richardson

Harrison Seuga photographed as requested

I Love You This Much
Felix Lucero

A few years before my daughter realized that she, in fact, is the one that knows everything, she still turned to me for all her important questions.

"Daddy," she would ask, "what's your favorite candy?" Of course later, like going from addition to calculus, her questions would become much harder to answer. But even when her questions were as abstruse as Socrates' apology, like "when you coming home, Daddy?" I still did not think she was capable of comprehending the complexity of a true response. "When you're a little bigger, Mi'ja," I'd say, the doubt in my voice as apparent as the doubt in her eyes. "I can't wait, Daddy," she'd say, and then she would spread her arms out as far as they could go and declare, "I love you this much, Daddy."

Building a strong bond between a child and a parent can be difficult under any circumstance, but it is especially arduous when they are apart. How many ways can you say I love you? How can you demonstrate that love in such a way that a child can understand it?

One afternoon, at the end of a very good visit, I walked with my daughter, hand in hand, to the spot where we always hug and say our good-byes. When we arrived, to my surprise, she kept tugging at my arm. "Take me over there," she said, pointing to the yellow line that separates two completely different worlds and where other people were also saying good-bye. Considering the line, which easily could have been a hundred light years away, I realized that it was not the distance that mattered to her, but only the fact that we could walk to the end of my world and the beginning of hers. "I love you this much, Daddy." Contemplating her words and out-stretched arms, I realized that my little girl showed me what I have desperately been trying to show her. How much "this much" actually is.

Be Careful What You Wish For
Michael McKenzie

Sticks and stones may break your bones, but words will never hurt you. I remember hearing my mother utter these very words each and every time she happened to hear one of my sisters making fun of me. And for a very long time I really believed words could never hurt me. But I've shed many tears because of some of the words I heard as a child. Sticks and stones may break your bones, but too many words hurt me.

By the time I turned four, silence became golden to me. It became a way for me to camouflage my terrible problems. Those close to me may have foreseen my dreadful stuttering enigma coming about, but to me it came out of nowhere like a bolt of lightning. I'll never forget this day, because it hit me like a crashing wave. I went to sleep one night, and when I woke up my mouth was broken.

My sisters just couldn't understand why I couldn't pronounce my words and called me names like "Duplicate," "Repeat," "Echo," and "Double Boo." But no matter where my mother was, or what she was doing—she could be in the kitchen cooking, in the middle of one of her and my four aunts' ritual dime tonk card games, in a heated conversation, or in the process of one of the sanctified ass kickings she gave me for hitting one of my sisters, because of something she said to me. Which with six older sisters happened an awful lot.

Whenever my mother heard one of my sisters making fun of me, before I could raise my fist to take revenge, my mother would immediately drop whatever she was doing and cut her eyes directly upon me. This look was not to be mistaken for her look that said, "Baby I'm so proud of you." Her ocean green eyes clearly said, "You better not even think about it, because if you do there will be hell to pay." Even though at that very moment revenge may have been my mission, protecting my own behind was a top priority, so her look would stop me dead in my tracks. I would stand there motionless with my mind saying, "But Momma." But my mouth saying, "Bububut Momomomma." As always her words were stern and crystal clear. "But Momma my ass. Boy how many times have I told you? Sticks and stones may break your bones, but words will never hurt you."

Whereas my mother overlooked my problem, and my sisters used it to their advantage, my grandmother, with her mass of tangled jet black curls, deep olive skin, and black opal eyes used to comfort me, and never ran out of kind words. She used to sit me down, and as I stared into her tender eyes, she would say to me, "Baby, the reason you fumble your words is because you are special. Your sisters don't know it, but you have a unique gift: your brain works faster than your mouth. And one day I'm going to take your gift from you, you just wait and see. You're going to look

Michael B. Willis's scar, photographed as requested

Jonathan Wilson reading at the poetry slam

up one day and your gift is going to be gone." Little did I know nine years later she would be right. At 13 my mind finally slowed down and allowed my mouth to catch up, and my terrible stuttering problem was gone. But so was my grandmother.

Venus Sinclair
A. Terrell Merritt

It happened on a Sunday, I remember that only because my mother and younger sister had gone to church. It was one of the rare occasions that she allowed my older brother and me to stay home. We were playing at the toxically polluted Calumet River with some of the other neighborhood kids. For decades, local steel mills used the Calumet for a dumpsite. We were always being told not to go into the water. We would walk across the river, balancing on pipelines that run feet above it, or "borrow" a rowboat from the mills and ride the river's current.

This particular Sunday, two weeks before I was to begin the fifth grade, we were crossing the pipelines when a freight train, going into the mills, rattled across the rickety wooden tracks overhead, startling a fourth grade classmate of mine, causing her to lose balance and spill into the river's contaminated depths. Unable to swim, she was whisked away by the overpowering current.

In total shock, we ran to get help. Hours passed before rescue divers finally dredged the frail, limp body of a ten-year-old girl, alive but comatose, from the putrid bowels of the unforgiving Calumet River. We took turns visiting our friend whom we wished would awaken so we all could be forgiven for not being on a church pew that unforgettable Sunday morning.

A week would pass before she made the decision that being in church on Sunday was not close enough to God as she would like to be. I can still hear Mrs. Ursell, my fifth grade teacher, taking attendance on the first day of school. "Ricky James?" "Here." "Alfonza Merritt?" "Here." "Kimberly Robinson?" "Here." "Venus Sinclair? Venus Sinclair? Venus Sinclair?"

Self-Doubt
William Packer

About a year and a half ago, I found myself in a really tough situation that challenged me to stand by the principles I'd preached for years. You see, I believe that prisons warehouse armies, and our strength lies in our cohesiveness. Black on black violence is strongly discouraged, and the emphasis is on what we share in common.

I was in North Kern State Prison at the time, Building #2. It was around 10am and I was playing a game of pinochle with three other guys, when a younger brother walked by the table in a really foul mood… He'd been in a funk recently, and couldn't seem to stay out of trouble. He was just returning from classification, where I was told he was informed of an imminent transfer and although he should've known it was a direct consequence of his latest disciplinary troubles, he was outraged.

Personally, I didn't really like "Truck" (that's the young brother's name.) He was all right, but there was something about him that I never warmed up to. Anyway, I asked him what was going on with him, and he angrily responded, "Don't say nothing to me, Cuz!" There was a challenge in his response, and before I could think about it, I heard myself saying, "What?!" Things get a little murky at this point, but I'll do the best I can to describe what happened next.

The entire time we were talking (some might say "posturing"), Truck had his hand in his pocket, and at some point he began gesturing like he had a shank. Truck is five foot nine, and weighs 160 pounds perhaps. I'm six three, and weigh a solid 270 pounds, so it made sense that he had to have a weapon, to be talking to me the way he was.

I should've let the whole thing go long before it got disrespectful, but a few of my old enemies – pride and ego – got involved, and wouldn't let me back out of it. So, there I was, standing in the dayroom, mad enough and wanting to kill Truck. Not for what he said to me (because I'd been there and done that before), but for what he'd made me feel. Doubt…

I'd been in for 16 years at that point. I'd been disciplinary free for four or five years, I'd been put up for transfer to San Quentin by the classification committee, where I'd be able to earn a college degree as well as the vocational training required of any serious lifer candidate desiring to be found suitable for parole. He made me ask myself: Do I throw away all of my progress and the years of sacrifice by my family, because I stuck my nose in someone else's business and got it stung? Or do I swallow my pride and walk away?

I chose family and progress.

Pride and ego are bitter pills to have to swallow. But for the sake of my family, my personal growth, and the idea that black on black violence is intolerable, I swallowed them both that day. It wasn't easy, and I straddled the fence a bit, but I got through it. Occasionally I think back on it, and play out the alternative course of action in my mind. Sometimes I even think I should've have handled it differently, but I know that's just self-doubt.

What happened that day was a very necessary step in a process that will prepare me for a successful reentry back into society. And since that day I've felt like I'm on the right path.

You Can't Hide Love!
Valeray Richardson

God rested on the seventh day after his world was completed. As a child growing up, I saw the true meaning of happiness when I saw the way my father loved my mother, sisters and brother. Together they raised five kids and showed true love to each other. I said to myself, "I want the same kind of marriage, love and joy as my parents." I was waiting for my world to be complete. May 20, 1995 I was to be married to the girl of my dreams, Ms. Shavonya Denise Jackson.

From the time I was a child, I knew that there was a God and I strongly believed in him. I've prayed for things as a child and believed God answered my prayers. "God, I pray in Jesus name that you bless my family, keep them all safe and in the arms of your protection. God I know I'm not always a good boy, but if you will allow for my father to get me and my brother a pair of motorcycles, I promise that I will be good. I also pray that everything my sister and brother asked for, they will receive. Amen." All my life I've prayed for things and I got many of them. Still till this day I will always believe in the power of prayer.

I met Shavonya at a Christmas party in 1992. From the first moment I saw her, I knew she was the lady God had made for me. She looked like she just dropped out of heaven. The way she moved across the room, swaying as she walked, had my heart skipping beats. Making my way toward her with nothing to lose, yet everything to gain, I asked her, "Would you like to dance with me?" With a beautiful smile, she said yes. This would be the first time I would hold her in my arms. We danced to the song by the Whispers, "Do They Turn You On." Holding her body next to mine, I made her promise me another dance before she walked out of my life. To my surprise she took me by the hand and lead me to a table for two. "This must be a match made in heaven," I thought to myself. We talked about everything and exchanged phone numbers. This girl was a goddess, her smile lit up my heart; the way she looked at me gave me a sense of real peace.

Things between Shavonya and me became stronger. We got an apartment together and shared special moments together. She would walk around the house with one of my shirts on. She truly looked sexy prancing around. She would be washing dishes and I would creep up on her dancing and singing to the record playing. When we made love she would love to lick me on the ears. That turned me on. We had this special bond that nobody could ever replace.

My family loved her and her family loved me. My oldest sister Shelia became close to Shavonya. They were like real sisters. They would talk on the phone for hours, go shopping, and do almost everything together. One day I was taking Shelia to the doctor. She told me, "Shavonya want to be your wife." I told her that I want her to be my wife and made plans to ask her. It was at Shelia's house when I asked Shavonya if she would make me complete, by being my wife. With tears in her eyes she said yes. I kissed her tears and then her soft lips. I made a promise in front of family and friends that I would always love, honor, respect her, and to be 100% faithful to her. She made me the same promise. We planned to raise a family, grow old together and be happy together forever.

Things were going well for us. The dreams we both shared were soon to become reality. We had everything planned out for our big day. Everything was paid for, the cake, rings, tuxes, and the reception hall.

May 14, 1995 is the day my dreams became a nightmare. Early that day I saw her beautiful smile for the last time. It was our final rehearsal before our big day. Kissing her, she and her best friend left. Seeing how happy she was made me very thankful for being the man whom she was glowing for. "See you at home Boo, I love you." "I love you too, baby."

While relaxing at home and cooking dinner, the phone rang. When I answered the phone I could hear it in Shavonya's mother's voice that something was wrong. "Mama what's wrong?" "Valeray! Shavonya and Trina were in a terrible car accident. They took them to Daniel Freeman Hospital in Inglewood. You need to get over there, baby."

Gathering my thoughts, I rushed to the hospital, praying the whole way there, asking God to let them be all right. When I arrived at the hospital, I felt this empty feeling come over me. Making my way through the door, Vikki, Shavonya's baby sister, met me. She was crying when she came toward me, hugging me tightly, she told me Shavonya passed away. They say a man isn't supposed to cry. I could not hold back my tears. I felt numb. Someone stole the love of my life. Making my way through the hospital I saw darkness. When I reached the room Shavonya was in, seeing her laying there with that white sheet covering her, I fell to my knees screaming, "God why? What did I do? Why did you give me her only to take her away from me?" I cussed God. I couldn't understand why.

My world became dark. I was bitter toward family and friends. I didn't want to be around anybody. I couldn't eat, sleep, nor go back into the home we had once shared. My sister Shelia came to me and said a prayer. "Vale, you know that God loves you. I love you too, Boo. I know you and Shavonya loved each other. God has called on her. I know she is in a better place, and she want you to be happy. You need to trust God. The funeral is in a couple of days and Ms. Jackson want you to be with her family." I started crying. "Do you believe in God's power?" "Yes I do." "I love you." "I love you too!"

One year later my sister Shelia passed away from cancer. I remember her words. God has called her home. Now he has called her to be with her sister Shavonya. I trust God and know that they are in heaven looking down on me.

Freedom???
Harrison Seuga

What is freedom? This seemingly simple question for someone who is 33 and has been incarcerated since the age of 17, is no longer as simple as the end of my incarceration.

When I was 15, I overdosed on cocaine after eating it in an attempt to get rid of incriminating evidence during a traffic stop. I chewed it up like unwanted vegetables, swallowing more than eating. My memories of the events leading up to my convulsions are of pure terror – a painful and haunting fear of dying. I held on to life with desperation, which probably induced the seizures and convulsions as my body merely simulated my inner struggles. It's like being in a dream and your body reflexively participating in sleep mode. It wasn't until I stopped being afraid and accepted death that the terror subsided.

What washed over me was the most peaceful feeling that I have ever experienced. A sort of transparency with no fears, worries, or complications – complete freedom, however fleeting. When I stopped being afraid, my heart stopped. I was resuscitated with a defibrillator and was told that my heart had stopped for about 60 seconds. Yet, in that time span, what I experienced was an absence of time, almost eternal – a dream that washed over me, like warm water against the skin. It's like closing your eyes in the shower and feeling the soothing warmth of warm water as it rolls along every surface of skin, caressing every nerve ending into absolute awareness.

The freedom from fear, from ignorance, has always proven elusive. My misconceptions of freedom led me to seek it through selling drugs, gangs, and stealing to find the freedoms I believed money could offer. In reality, I had begun to build my prison around and in me – mentally, years before I got to Pelican Bay State Prison at 18 years old.

Seven years later, at the age of 25, I found myself back in Pelican Bay. I had just gotten out of the security housing unit (SHU), the modern term for the "hole." I was sent there for assaulting an inmate during a riot while I was at Calipatria State Prison. It was at this time, about eight years into my incarceration, that I truly began to free myself. I existed in a state of fear – driving my belief that the only way I would make it out of prison alive was to accept the use of violence, to avoid being the victim of violence. Fear does many things to an individual, imprisoning one's consciousness, again the terror as I described earlier – like the fear of dying or in this case, the fear of being killed. Yet unlike the terror I felt when I overdosed, this occurred over a prolonged period of time, almost ten years.

I was 15, locked up in juvenile hall for selling cocaine to an undercover police. I was told during a visit that a close friend of mine had gotten killed. "Seco." Someone drove up beside his car as he was parking and blew off the side of his face with a shotgun at close range. I had been shot at before – had other close friends shot or killed around me. But this seemed so different. I was not going to be Seco. I foolishly believed that violence would free me from violence.

It took a conscious decision to accept death or being killed – like when I overdosed – to be free. To free myself from the lingering effects of fear at its most intimate junction. To both love life and accept the end of life as inevitable, not something to fear but to accept, that like true love it is neither possessed nor lost. It is not an easy decision, but it is a choice. I choose to accept that death would be simpler to accept than reciprocating the violence that I believed was necessary to live. It does not change the fact that I do not want to die in prison, away from loved ones, but I do not want to be imprisoned by such fears.

Yet, like the words that breathe life – my life – into these pages as I write, it is a direct result of my education. Freedom and education are often synonymous. It is through my education that I realize my connectedness, my humanness, my humanity…

Education ultimately has afforded me the knowledge that has helped me to secure my freedom, from my own self-contained prisons, my fears. Ignorance seems to breed many things, least of all a freedom. One semester I took a sociology class at San Quentin's Patten College Program, for my Associate of Arts degree. Near the end of the semester, I asked the teacher a question. "Now that we grasp and understand the process of socialization, possess the knowledge of stratification, the structuralization of economics and gender in relation to poverty and inequalities, what can we do about it? We just learned how small and powerless we are in relation to this monstrous machine – more so as prisoners. What is the point of knowing something if we are powerless to do anything about it?"

I don't remember her exact words, but I interpreted in this way:

"By grasping its mechanisms, you are better prepared to recognize and address its flaws. There are many points of influencing change throughout its machinery; every bolt and spring influences its overall productivity. Sometimes it is the smallest things that influence the biggest changes. When your world view changes, the world around you changes also."

A Message from Beyond
Paul Uribe

He came to me in a dream not long after I had been imprisoned—at a time when I questioned my own fortitude, struggled with my past, contemplated a seemingly bleak future, the purpose of life…

Mist-laden salted winds blow into my senses while a rain soaked body slowly comes into focus. His dripping white knuckles clench the bars of my cell door, his face pressed tight against them, bloodshot eyes peering in. Harshness enters my world of slumber with spittle and course awareness. "PAUL, COME OUT!"

Surprisingly calm, I rise up in my bunk rubbing at my eyes in disbelief. Lowering myself to the floor, my bare feet come in contact with wet concrete. I look down at them as I become more conscious of the impossible activity taking shape outside my 4' x 10' enclosure.

On the other side of my cell door, some distance off, my uncle is beckoning to me from his ghostly white Boston Whaler. Behind him the vast expanse of the pacific North Coast waters loom. There is an unnatural quiet darkness as increased commotion of sea and cloud commence. Wind begins to blow rain diagonally as he moves aft to lash down a flapping canvas. Then rising, he turns to me, arms open wide, palm out, in invitation.

The last time I saw my uncle Elwin alive, my father and I were standing in the waiting room of Sutter Memorial hospital. Alone together we watched as my aunt pushed him in his wheelchair through the heavy double doors, and into a section of the facility where we could not go.

Just before the doors swung closed, his arm shot up above her shoulder with a thumbs up gesture, then he was gone. Absorbed within the gleaming white walls, chrome fixtures, and the smell of disinfectant. For a moment, the vaulted ceiling echoed some disturbing surreal quietness as other patients and staff carried out their duties – unaware, unaffected. It all seemed so offhand.

I flashed on what I knew of my uncle. He grew up on the sea, had been a decorated pilot of WWII, and after that a commercial fisherman until about two years before his death. He lived as he would, by his own code. I'm told that in his younger years he was quite a hell-raiser. Worked hard…and drank hard, and in the end I'm pretty sure that's what got the best of him.

We really weren't very close during my youth. He was 40 years my senior, but I respected him because he had treated my older brother so well – raised him, in a manner of speaking. His experience had trickled down, and it later occurred to me that a great deal of my identity as a man of the sea, a fisherman, a deep-sea diver, was sparked by influence alone.

Now staring out of my dingy cell in boxers, and bare feet, I shake as my heart begins to pound and he continues to beckon me aboard.

As his arms rise I hear the breakers roar and find myself in the forecastle at the anchor windlass. Suddenly, I become anxious with awareness at the imposing closeness of the jagged coastal cliffs. Instinctively knowing my job, I engage the winch, hoist anchor, and slowly we move away from the unprotected cove.

My position is forward and aloft as is usual, scanning any obstacles in front of the sixty foot vessel until we are well clear of the treacherous California coast. For now, this is all that is important – this is my purpose.

Coming about on a southward, amidships my uncle moves with specific intent, reading the signs of current, he puts us on a course parallel to the heavy black clouds in the distance. Outriggers down, lines baited, his is a working vessel.

Years on the sea have made the skin of his face tanned and course. Crevices of experience and concern move about with his mood. He's not know to be a gentle man or one to mince words – his hands are evidence of a man who has known hard, but mostly honest work. Hands that have also been known to turn quickly into tools of punishment.

Well underway, the Boston Whaler rises on the waves with baited lines trailing at a rate suitable for attracting salmon. While three miles to the east, the rain forest of Mendocino coast lie misted, waiting.

From my position aloft, I drop to the deck and make my way aft to the fantail, unconsciously timing my steps to meet the cadence of the rolling waves. I find my uncle Elwin pulling a bucket of baitfish from the live well. I sit across from him and begin threading herring onto large hooks. I start to ask him, "Elwin, how the…" but he just looks at me from beneath bushy eyebrows and slowly shakes his head.

As is common in dreamscapes and nightmares, certain things are understood. Returning to his work, without a word the message was clear. All that is important now is the present – the task at hand.

Elwin has come to build a fire under me – to remind me of who I am, of where I'm from. To show me I'm not alone, that I'm being watched and that what I do counts.

Time eclipses and fog begins to roll in as I am forced to endure an uncomfortable quietness wrought of my uncle's malice. Nothing is expected of me but hard work and perseverance. I notice his nostrils widen as he smells the air. His movements become calculated while he turns the vessel due north – back towards the storm from which we have come, to cut another cross-section of his trusted fishing grounds.

I go below deck for soundings and when I return topside I notice a difference in his demeanor. As the waters rise his face grows stern, the lines hard, but in his eyes there is a strange mischief. It strikes me that he is excited in a fierce kind of way, that he welcomes an impending struggle – he is thrilled with the thought that the risk of living is upon him. Standing at the helm, his head rolls back and I hear him laugh in contempt of the approaching storm—he is challenging destiny and is unafraid. This is his message to me.

I see him still, standing there like David before the presence of monstrous Goliath. As the fog overtakes us, he reaches into the pocket of his foul weather jacket and produces a harmonica. He begins to play a tune from his generation, the generation of my parents. I recognize the song and close my eyes to the soothing rhythm. The vessel drops off into a trough between the waves, and I bounce hard, fully awake in my prison bunk, but for a moment I can still vaguely hear the music and smell the last traces of salted wind. At first I'm a bit unsettled in the eeriness of the twilight, then the feeling becomes one of comfort. I feel empowered – and a little less alone.

Charlie K. Complex Awakens from a Long Nap
Michael B. Willis

Humiliated, that's the word that best defines how I felt sitting there covered with raw eggs on my face, in my hair and all over my work clothes, with their single word echoing in my head like it was some sort of mantra: "Nigger!" How can one single six-letter word wield so much power, contempt and cause so much pain? Words can create dichotomies. Express enigmas. So it is our words that condemn us, revealing our true nature. I was 16 years of age, trying to earn a living working at Church's Chicken in Cicero, Illinois. Monday through Friday, I rode three buses for two hours to work and home. I had made the choice of working instead of attending school so that I could avoid living in foster homes.

After being beaten while tied to a steel beam in the basement numerous times, having my head scalded with boiling hot water, and escaping molestation on several occasions, I was unwilling to endure any further parental supervision. I did what I felt was necessary for my well being. I sold marijuana, valiums (Roche twos, fives, and tens) and I paid a fine looking woman named Nature to pay my rent. I'd give her $50.00 every month and smoke weed with her and she'd be content. I worked hard every day, so much so, that one night I dreamt that it was raining drumsticks.

On this particular night, as I sat awaiting my bus's arrival (it wasn't due for another 21 minutes), I noticed the beige and white station wagon as it began to decelerate the closer it got to my bus stop. The windows on both sides were rolled down and four bodies balanced themselves like acrobats out of them as I was greeted with their loathing and a barrage of eggs. It seemed that none of them managed to miss me. I sat there dumbfounded, awaiting my bus's arrival. (I still find that I am unable to fathom why they felt that I warranted this treatment.)

So, what was the origin of their feelings of hatred towards me? I didn't know them, nor did they know me. I have given this a considerable amount of thought. Believe me. Should I hate them? Seek revenge? No. Why should I assassinate my character and integrity at someone else's expense?

Then another thought came to me. Maybe they didn't truly understand why they hated me either. Possible they were the unfortunate victims of their parents' indoctrination—scary thought.

Finally, the bus arrived. As I got on the bus everyone grew silent, all eyes were upon me. My legs were rooted and I was numb. Adorned in my new wardrobe of eggshells and egg-yolks, for the record, I was not trying to make a fashion statement. At this moment, I realized that the only two blacks on this bus were myself and the bus driver. I averted my eyes and discovered that the long seat in the rear of the bus was vacant. As I headed towards my seat, I could feel their eyes upon me, and hear the buzz of their whispers. Once there, I seated myself and stared blackly out the window into the night. Since this time, I have become consciously aware of the sad reality that our world has become more populated by its biases than its empathy.

The Best Time in My Life
Jonathan Wilson

When I was younger during the summer on the weekends when I wanted some money, I would often time go to the park across the street from where we lived to find my Dad. He would normally be sitting in the park on the benches along with his friends drinking and watching the softball game. I found this to be an opportune time in which to ask for a little bit more money than usual because Dad would be in front of his friends and didn't want to appear cheap. If Dad appeared hesitant or even complained one of his friends would surely say, "Give that boy some money," or they would offer some themselves. My dad would have a little smile on his face and say, "You think you're slick," and then hand me a crisp $20.00 bill that he pulled from a small roll of bills tucked away in the secret part of his wallet. Before he handed the bill over he'd rub the bill back and forth between his thumb and forefinger just to make sure there weren't two bills stuck together.

Softball games were played every weekend between a lounge he hung out in named Nick's and any other lounge that had a team. Actually the official name of his lounge was the Caddy Inn, which is the name the team had embroidered on their jerseys. However most people that frequented the place knew it by the owner's name, which was Nick.

Nick's was located just three blocks from where he lived and was like a second home to Dad and many of his friends who seemed to always be there whenever I'd go there with him. Rain, sleet or snow, hot or cold, Nick's doors would always be open. So on the day the team wasn't playing and I couldn't find him in the park, it was a sure bet that he'd be there. Often times, when my Dad and I would hang out, which was mostly on Saturdays, we'd often time end the day by stopping by at Nick's. I can't remember a time that either one of us weren't greeted when we walked in. Although operated as a business, Nick's was a place that made you feel automatically welcomed when you came in. Like a shelter from a storm, if you were troubled by anything Nick's seemed to have an environment that was capable of instantly lightening the load. It seemed the more you came, the more you became attached. You were more than just a person buying a drink. You also slowly became part of the goings on there. So I guess this is why the place felt so cohesive.

The place was usually packed with a few seats available left open at the bar. There was people from all walks of life and professions at Nick's at any given time. White-collar workers and blue-collar workers alike. Some sidewalk sellers would come in if Nick allowed them to peddle their wares. On any given weekend, one could buy anything from diamond rings to an automobile. If you felt lucky you could place a bet on a horse running in any of the races throughout the day. You didn't need to be at the Aqueduct or Bay Meadows. All you needed to know was the name, number of the horse, what race he runs and, the most important thing the odds. Depending on the amount bet, the odds determined how much you'd be paid if you won. It seemed almost everyone felt lucky because everyone would play a number. Some days my Dad would even ask me for numbers. And although Dad never got rich, at least as far as I could tell, he was very lucky and would pick the right horses most of the time. I remember once him placing a bet and receiving the little yellow slip of paper which was an actual receipt from the number runner. Later that afternoon I remember him smiling and many of his friends patting him on the back because he had picked the right combination of numbers. They called it a straight. The number man walked in and came over to where I was sitting with my Dad and pulled out a faded yellow envelope stuffed with bills. My Dad smiled and said, "thank you."

He then counted the money, took some bills out and said, "I want 1-6-2 in the second race, and 7-3-5 in the third," while giving it back to the number runner, who then glanced around very quickly and pulled an enormous roll of money out of his pocket and added those bills to the top of it. He then pulled out a small pad from his jacket pocket, wrote Dad's numbers down on a page that looked to be filled with many other numbers and initials. He then reached in his other pocket and took out another pad that resembled the actual roll of paper that is used for receipts when you purchase something by credit card. He wrote the number down again on the outer white paper and then pulled the yellow one off and gave it to Dad. All this took about 30-45 seconds.

Once their business was completed and the runner left, I asked my Dad what kind of job the number runner had since it seemed he was always very sharply dressed, wore nice jewelry, and drove a new car, usually a Cadillac. Dad must have read my mind because he then gave me a crisp $100.00 bill. He told me to be careful and not spend it all at once. He also said, "Son, that job is not for you, get a real job." I asked him, "A real job like yours?" He replied, "No, you should become a dentist." I never became a dentist, but I have since inherited the same sort of luck Dad had with games of chance.

During those long hot summer days, while walking by Nick's, I would often time peek in the window before stopping in to use the bathroom. As soon as I opened the door, it felt as if a blast of arctic wind hit me as I stepped into the dark, air-conditioned lounge. Upon hearing the door open, Nick would stop what he was doing, look up from behind the bar, give me a wave and say, "Hi little Johnny." I would feel very privileged because adolescents were never allowed in a lounge absent a parent. However, because of my Dad I had carte blanche. After using the bathroom and on my way out, Nick would always call me over to the bar where he would have an ice-cold glass of Coca Cola waiting for me. This wasn't just any glass of Coca Cola; it seemed as if he took particular care in making it. He would only use crushed ice and put a cherry on the top and throw in a stirring straw. Cold sweat would be running down the side of the glass. I'd climb on to a stool and slowly sip my Coke through the stirring straw while my eyes finally adjusted to the dim lighting inside.

There were small bowls of Spanish peanuts, the ones with the red skins still on them, strategically placed on the semi-circle counter which made up the center of the bar. I would eat small handfuls of peanuts and occasionally dropped them in my Coke. As I listened to the jukebox, which seemed to always be on, my body swayed with the beat of, "you are my starship." The combination of music, soft lights, cool air, and the smell of alcohol which permeated the air along with the taste of Coca Cola would always place me in a dreamy euphoric like state. I could sit that way uninterrupted for hours. I would spend anywhere between 20-30 minutes watching Nick go about his daily duties which seemed to consist mostly of wiping glasses off and then putting them up to the light to ensure that he had gotten all the smudges off them. His other duties, which he always seemed to be doing, would be stocking the bar with bottles of liquor and beer and cleaning the counter of the bar. But one afternoon I

discovered what his real job was and I could tell he liked it from the way he did it.

One afternoon as the lounge became crowded, I watched Nick begin to make drinks. This was where his real talent lay. Like a juggler in a circus, he began to flip bottles over and pour liquor. Like a chemist, he quickly mixed different colors of fluids together in glasses. He'd pour each fluid to an exact predetermined amount and fill each glass to the rim. He would then slide the glass along the bar over to the customer. I've seen him slide a glass maybe ten to 15 feet and not spill a drop of alcohol. It seemed as if he could take what seemed to be hundreds of orders at a time. I don't know how he heard half the orders that were shouted to him over all the music and commotion in the bar, but as far as I know he remembered them all. Since then I have developed a deep respect for those who bartend.

As the years passed by and I relocated to California, I became disconnected with Nick's and many of my family and friends. Many things in my life have now transpired. Two things, like a thorn in my side, stay with me. For one, my dad is no longer living, a fact that pains me greatly. However, I have faith that one day we'll be together again. Secondly, Nick's is no longer there. My sister having had to travel back to Brooklyn to attend my dad's funeral was jointly responsible for following my dad's last three requests. Of these three requests, the most important one it seemed, only because he told me countless times, was his cremation. He would say, "Boy – you are my only son and it will be your responsibility to have me cremated when I die." At that time in my life, not really wanting to acknowledge the reality of it, I just listened. I remember feeling very worried that something was about to happen to him, and not really knowing what to say I would ask him, "Why?" He would then reply, "Cemeteries are eye sores and a waste of valuable land; they should build parks and schools for children, not have bodies there." At first I was horrified at the notion of this but in time I have found wisdom in this thought.

The other request was to have his ashes spread around at Nick's which was nothing but a vacant lot now. Since I was unable to do this myself, having been told countless times, I wondered whether or not his last request would be fulfilled. I knew much more than anyone else how very important this last request was. It is a troubling thought on my mind to this day not to have been able to carry out his last request after being enlisted to do so. I hope he understands. The only comfort I receive in this area is my sister assuring me that it was done.

I try to imagine in my mind how the corner of Troy and Atlantic Avenues might look without Nick's. I cannot envision it. Maybe I don't want to. Dad was strongly bonded to Nick's while alive, so strongly bonded that after his death and cremation, he wanted ashes from his body to be part of the landscape. I feel, at least in a symbolic way, that there is a connection with Dad's death and the absence, or more appropriate, the death of Nick's. I think about the eventuality of death that we as human beings move towards as well as the eventual demise of institutions and establishments. I wonder whether these two things are somehow intimately connected in some cosmic way that evokes similar feelings in me once they're gone? And if connected, just how important the memories of these things are? I'll leave these thoughts and questions for the great minds of another day.

For me now, as I struggle with many painful memories of the past and what was the "best time in my life," I can even now still taste the combination of Spanish peanuts and ice cold Coca Cola as I sip it through a stirring straw. And every time I hear Ray Charles sing, "Georgia on my mind," the song that was to be played at his wake per his second request, although it causes me to cry, I also hear Dad telling me, "Don't cry over me, I lived a good life." And although the years continue to march forward and I miss him more—I also miss Nick's. What I've come to know is that the death of a loved one and the death of an era are equally sad. But even now, at this very moment when I think of Dad and Nick's, both will always be there for me.

In loving memory of the late John N. Wilson Sr.

About the Prison University Project

The Prison University Project is a non-profit organization whose mission is to provide high-quality higher education to people incarcerated at San Quentin State Prison; to generate public support for prison education and recovery programs; and to increase public awareness about criminal justice issues nationwide.

The San Quentin College Program is supported by the Prison University Project and is the only on-site, degree-granting higher education program in California's prison system. As of May 2008, 69 students had earned their associate of arts degrees at San Quentin. Many students parole before completing the degree and continue their education on the outside.

To find out more about the work of the Prison University Project, please visit *prisonuniversityproject.org*.